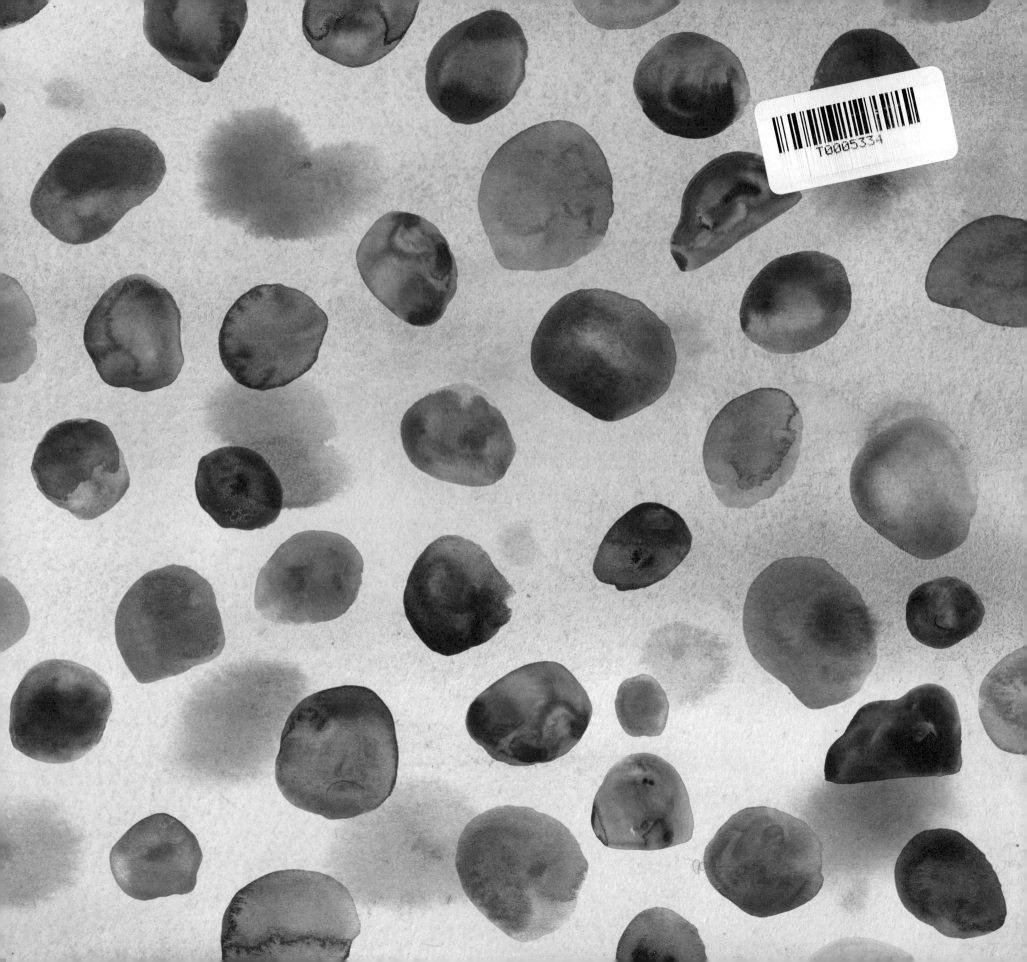

For my parents, with love
—L. B. B.

For Elouan
—M. M.

MARGARET K. McELDERRY BOOKS
An imprint of Simon & Schuster Children's Publishing Division
1230 Avenue of the Americas, New York, New York 10020
Text © 2023 by Leslie Barnard Booth
Illustration © 2023 by Marc Martin
Book design by Sonia Chaghatzbanian © 2023 by Simon & Schuster, Inc.
MARGARET K. McELDERRY BOOKS is a trademark of Simon & Schuster, Inc.
For information about special discounts for bulk purchases, please contact Simon & Schuster Special Sales at 1-866-506-1949 or
business@simonandschuster.com.
The Simon & Schuster Speakers Bureau can bring authors to your live event. For more information or to book an event, contact the Simon & Schuster
Speakers Bureau at 1-866-248-3049 or visit our website at www.simonspeakers.com.
The text for this book was set in Bodoni.
The illustrations for this book were rendered in watercolor.
Manufactured in China
0423 SCP
First Edition
10 9 8 7 6 5 4 3 2 1
Library of Congress Cataloging-in-Publication Data
Names: Barnard Booth, Leslie, author. | Martin, Marc, illustrator.
Title: A stone is a story / Leslie Barnard Booth ; illustrated by Marc Martin.
Description: First edition. | New York : Margaret K. McElderry Books, 2023. | Includes bibliographical references. | Audience: Ages 4–8 |
Audience: Grades 2–3 | Summary: "A stone is not just a stone. A stone is a story. Journey across history to see how one stone changes and transforms,
from magma, oozing under Earth's crust, to sand ground down by a rushing river, to the heart of a mountain. Watch what happens when rain, ice,
and wind mold this rock into something new, something you might even hold in your hand, and imagine all that is left for the stone to become.
Leslie Barnard Booth weaves captivating prose to answer one of kids' most curious questions, 'where do rocks come from?', brought to colorful
life by Marc Martin's stunning illustrations"–Provided by publisher.
Identifiers: LCCN 2022030671 (print) | LCCN 2022030672 (ebook) | ISBN 9781534496941 (hardcover) | ISBN 9781534496958 (ebook)
Subjects: LCSH: Rocks—Juvenile literature. | Petrology—Juvenile literature. | Geology—Juvenile literature.
Classification: LCC QE432.2.B37 2023 (print) | LCC QE432.2 (ebook) | DDC 552—dc23/eng20221129
LC record available at https://lccn.loc.gov/2022030671
LC ebook record available at https://lccn.loc.gov/2022030672

A Stone Is a Story

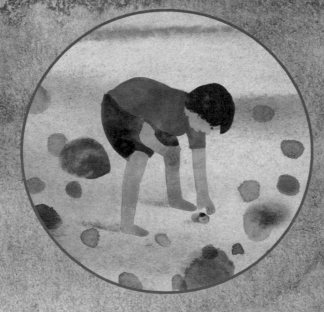

written by Leslie Barnard Booth

illustrated by Marc Martin

Margaret K. McElderry Books
New York London Toronto Sydney New Delhi

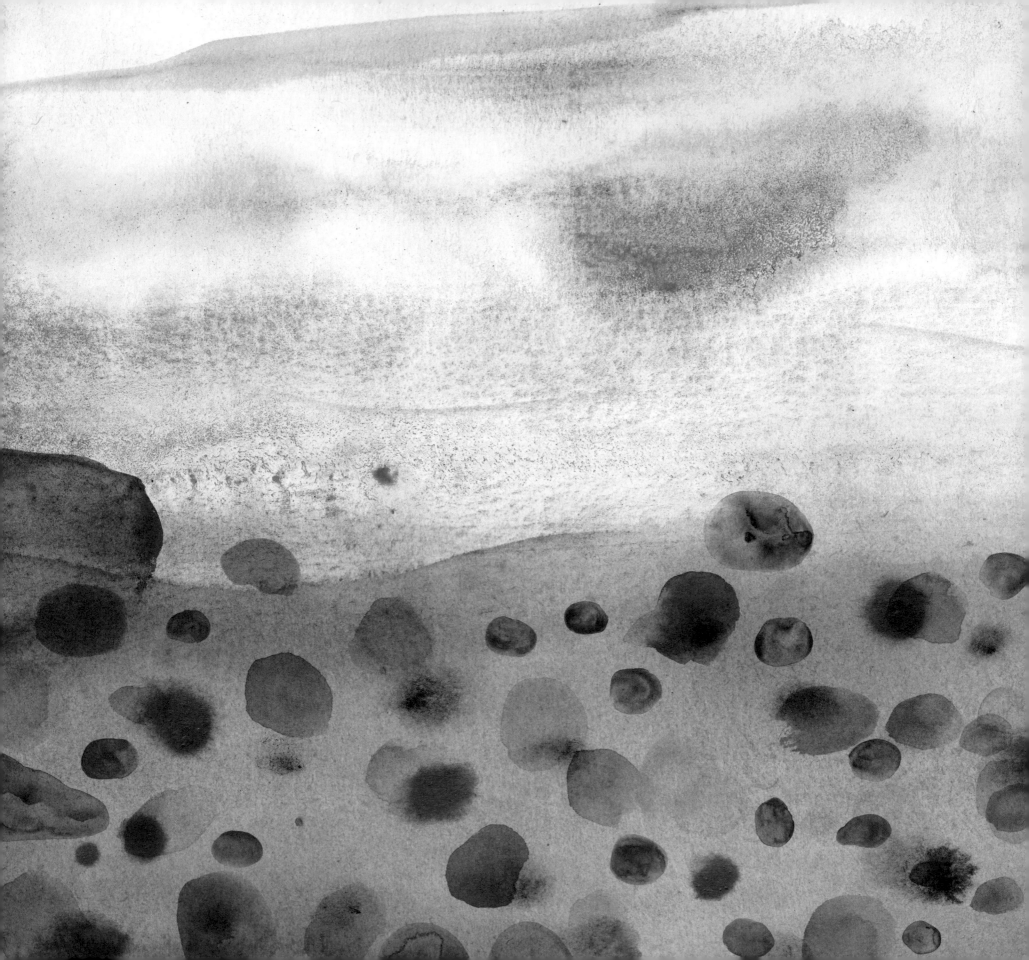

A
stone
is not
just a stone.

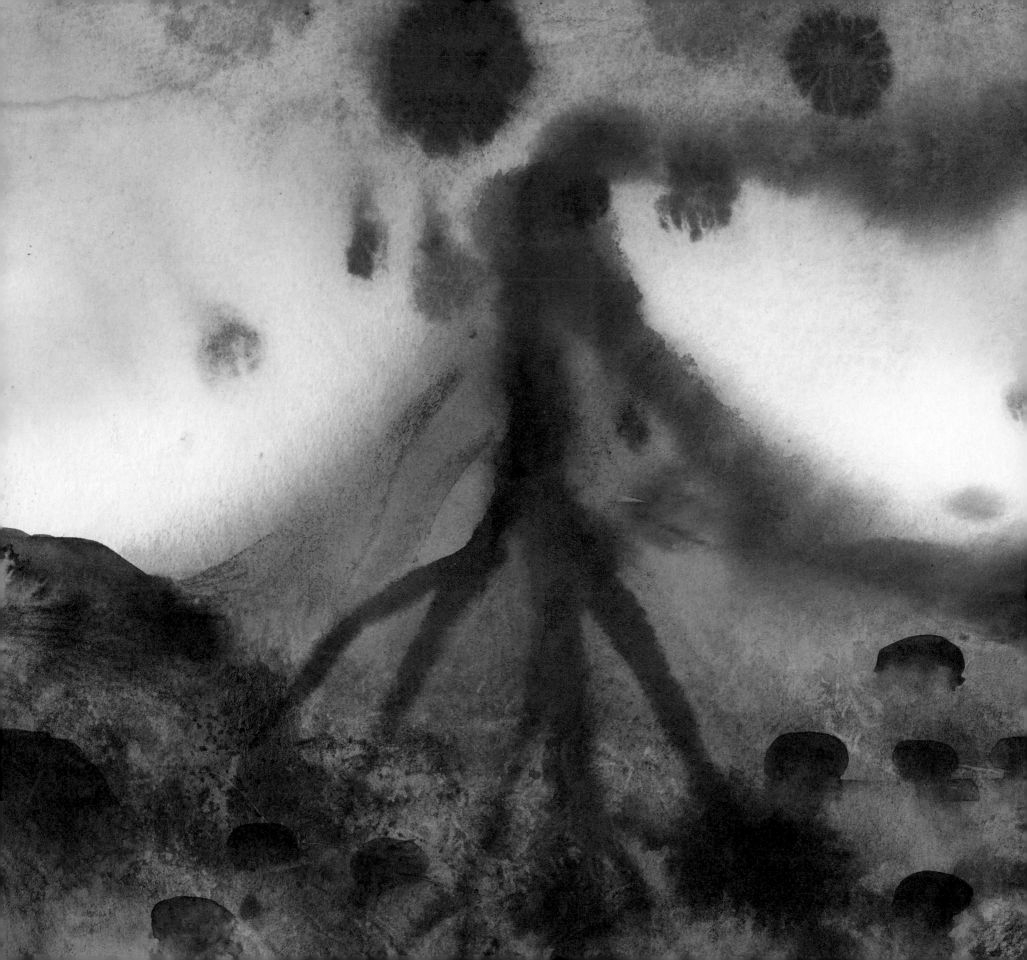

A stone has slipped
tumbled
crumbled

crashed.
And on that day . . .

A stone is a story.

A stone has been magma, oozing under Earth's crust.

A stone has been lava, gushing from the mouth of a volcano.

A stone has been wrenched apart by roots.

Crushed and dragged by a glacier.

Swept up in the foam of a rushing river.

Molded.

Carved.

Ground down to a speck of sand
and sent to sea.

There
it has waited
for millions of years.

Bits of seaweed and shell and bone
have piled on top of it
have become part of it.

A stone has felt the slow drifting
the slow   shifting

of the surface of the earth.

A stone has been driven
down
down
down
into deep
searing
darkness.

Squeezed and scorched,
it has *transformed*.

Eras have passed.
Ages have flown.
The dinosaurs have come
                    and gone.

Cave lions have prowled.

Mammoths have grazed.

The first humans have made the first music.

And a stone?

Thrust upward,
skyward,
    a stone has risen
        high
            into the heart of a mountain—
a mountain whittled by wind
by rain
by ice
by time.

A stone has been a ledge
on the edge
of a cliff.
A stone has been scuffed and scraped.

Maybe *you* find a stone.

You might pick it up.

You might turn it in your hand.
You might see the parts of the stone
that were once lava
that were once sand
that were once bone.

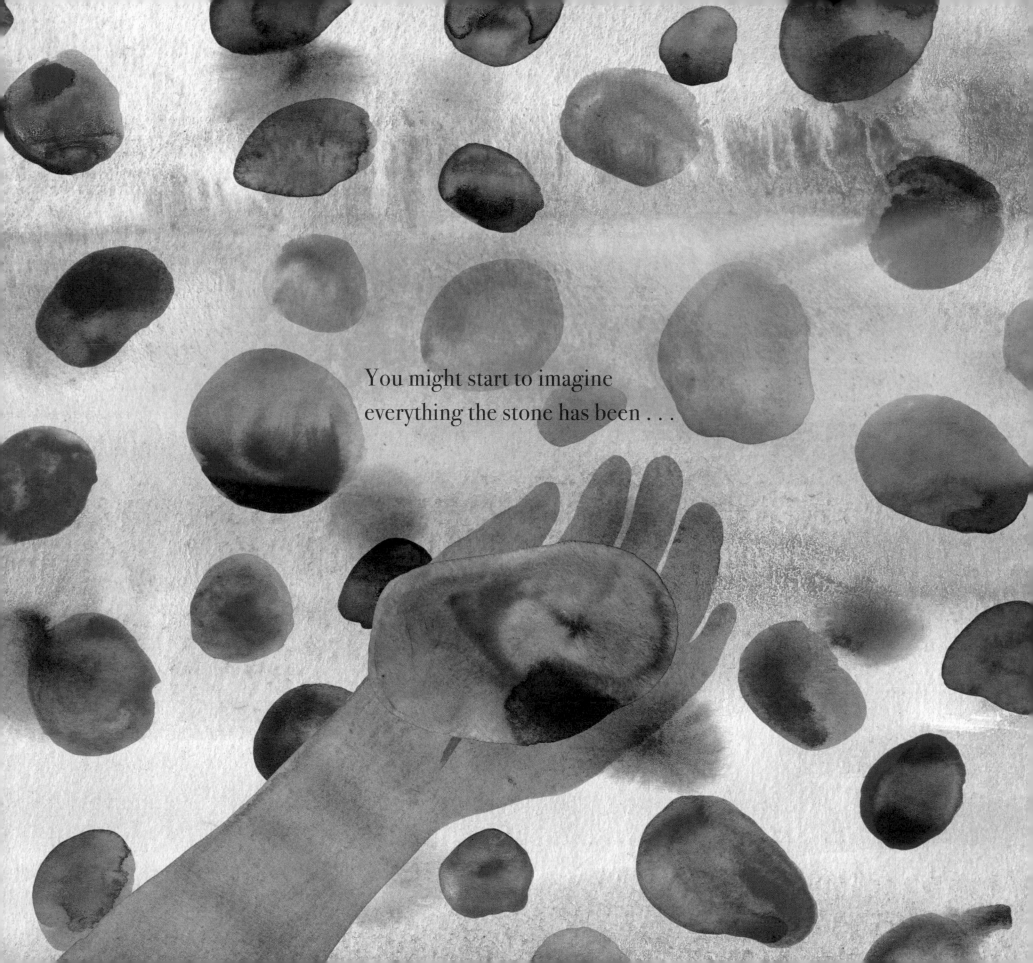

You might start to imagine
everything the stone has been . . .

and all it might become.

Rocks: Not Set in Stone

Wait a minute. So, rocks *move around*? And *transform*? And *tell stories*? Yes, yes, and yes! Though most people think of rocks as stable and permanent, natural forces are continuously moving them around and altering their size, shape, and structure. Because a rock's physical form reflects its history, rocks can tell stories about Earth's distant past and about the formation of the landscapes we see today.

Geologists (scientists who study the earth) divide rocks into three main types based on how they formed. These three types are igneous, sedimentary, and metamorphic. As a rock experiences different forces and events, it transforms from one type into another. This ongoing process of change is called the rock cycle. There is no set order to the rock cycle, and each type of rock can transform into any other type at any point in time.

Igneous

At extremely high temperatures, rock can melt, becoming a liquid. Igneous rock forms when this scorching-hot liquid rock cools and solidifies. But how does rock get hot enough to melt? The answer lies deep belowground.

Our planet consists of three main layers, and the temperature of these layers increases with depth. Earth's coolest, outermost layer is called the crust. Made of solid rock, the crust is home to all living things—including you! At Earth's center is its dense, blazing hot, ball-shaped core. Between the crust and the core lies the mantle, Earth's largest layer.

Cooler than the core and hotter than the crust, Earth's mantle is made of semisolid rock. It also contains pockets of hot liquid rock, called magma. Sometimes magma rises through the mantle and enters the crust. It melts surrounding rocks and mixes with them. Trapped underground, this mixture cools and hardens *slowly*, producing igneous rocks with large, visible grains, like granite or gabbro. Other times magma surges up through Earth's crust and bursts onto the surface as lava. This is what's happening when a volcano erupts! Bathed in cool air, the lava solidifies *quickly*. There isn't time for large grains to develop. Instead, the lava transforms into a fine-grained igneous rock, such as rhyolite or basalt.

Sedimentary

Loose bits of natural material that accumulate on or near Earth's surface are called sediment. Sand, pebbles, and boulders are all examples of sediment. Sediment also includes plant and animal remains, such as leaves or shells. When sediment is deeply buried, it can join together and harden, forming sedimentary rock.

New sediment is constantly being produced and transported across Earth's surface. Burrowing animals weaken and dislodge rocks. Gravity causes rocks to fall and shatter. Rivers, glaciers, and sand-charged winds grind rocks down, carry bits of them away, and deposit these bits in new places. Over time these deposits grow. Newer layers bury older layers. The weight of this additional material packs the lower layers down, squeezing out gaps between grains.

As water circulates through any remaining openings, it leaves behind minerals. These minerals act like cement, joining the grains together to form a solid whole.

Examples of sedimentary rocks include sandstone (made of sand), mudstone (made of mud), coal (made of ancient plant remains), and limestone (made of the shells and skeletons of ocean organisms).

Metamorphic

If a rock experiences extreme heat, extreme pressure, or both—but stops short of melting—it can transform, or metamorphose, into metamorphic rock. When a rock metamorphoses, both its minerals and texture can change. As a result, the new rock may look nothing like the original. Metamorphic rocks develop much deeper belowground than sedimentary rocks. In fact, they typically form *many miles* beneath Earth's surface, in the lower crust or upper mantle. At this depth, temperatures are sizzling hot. Due to the enormous weight of the rocks above, pressure is extremely high too.

Interestingly, the same process that produces mountain ranges also produces huge amounts of metamorphic rock. Here's how it works. Together, Earth's crust and uppermost mantle form our planet's rigid outer shell, which is broken into dozens of pieces called tectonic plates. These giant slabs of rock drift over the hotter, softer part of the mantle at the very slow rate of about one to two inches per year. Where they meet, tectonic plates sometimes ram into each other, squeezing massive quantities of rock both upward *and* downward. Aboveground this bunched-up rock forms a mountain range. The rock that plunges belowground gets scrunched, squashed, and baked. In short, it metamorphoses!

Marble is metamorphosed limestone. Slate is metamorphosed shale. Even metamorphic rocks can metamorphose! For example, if slate is exposed to increasing pressure and heat, it turns into phyllite—another type of metamorphic rock.

Now go forth and do what geologists do!

Step outside, look around, and start asking questions about the rocks and landscapes in your part of the world.

Additional resources available at lesliebarnardbooth.com.

Glossary

Core: Earth's extremely hot, iron-rich, ball-shaped center

Crust: Earth's outermost layer, made of solid rock

Geologist: a scientist who studies Earth—what it's made of, what forces shape it, and how it transforms over time

Glacier: huge sheet of ice and packed snow that is present year-round and flows very slowly under the force of its own weight

Igneous rock: rock formed when magma or lava cools and hardens

Lava: melted rock that erupts at Earth's surface

Magma: melted rock below Earth's surface

Mantle: Earth's largest layer, found between the crust and the core

Metamorphic rock: rock that has changed due to extreme heat, extreme pressure, or a combination of both, while remaining solid

Metamorphose: (of rock) to undergo a change in texture and/or mineral content while remaining solid

Minerals: naturally occurring, solid substances that make up Earth's rocks, sands, and soils

Organism: a living thing

Rock: a naturally occurring, solid mass made up of minerals

Rock cycle: a series of events through which rocks continuously transform, turning from one type into another, and another, indefinitely

Sediment: naturally occurring, solid grains—such as sand, shells, pebbles, and boulders—that are not attached to one another

Sedimentary rock: rock formed when sediment joins together and solidifies

Tectonic plates: massive pieces of Earth's crust and uppermost mantle that drift very slowly over the softer, hotter mantle rock beneath

Volcano: a vent in Earth's surface through which lava, ash, gas, and rock fragments escape

Selected Sources

Grotzinger, John P., and Thomas Jordan. *Understanding Earth*. 7th ed. New York: W. H. Freeman, 2014.

Marshak, Stephen. *Essentials of Geology*. 5th ed. New York: W. W. Norton & Company, 2016.

McPhee, John. *Annals of the Former World*. New York: Farrar, Straus and Giroux, 2000.

Prinz, Martin, George Harlow, and Joseph Peters, eds. *Simon & Schuster's Guide to Rocks and Minerals*. New York: Simon & Schuster, 1978.

Special thanks to geologists Dr. Adam M. Booth and Dr. Scott Burns
of Portland State University for consulting on this book.

Thanks as well to Literary Arts, whose support helped bring this book into being.